Ice Skating

B A S I C S

Ice Skating

BASICS

AARON FOESTE

Photographed by Bruce Curtis

Sterling Publishing Co., Inc. New York

Library of Congress Cataloging-in-Publication Data

Foeste, Aaron.
    Ice skating basics / Aaron Foeste ; photographed by Bruce Curtis.
       p.   cm.
    Includes index.
    ISBN 0-8069-9517-3
    1. Skating. 2. Skating—Study and teaching. I. Title.
  GV849.F574   1998
  796.91—dc21   98-21163
                                        CIP

Designed by Judy Morgan

1   3   5   7   9   10   8   6   4   2

First paperback edition published in 2000 by
Sterling Publishing Company, Inc.
387 Park Avenue South, New York, N.Y. 10016
© 1998 by Aaron Foeste photographed by Bruce Curtis
Distributed in Canada by Sterling Publishing
% Canadian Manda Group, One Atlantic Avenue, Suite 105
Toronto, Ontario, Canada M6K 3E7
Distributed in Great Britain and Europe by Chris Lloyd
463 Ashley Road, Parkstone, Poole, Dorset, BH14 0AX, England
Distributed in Australia by Capricorn Link (Australia) Pty Ltd.
P.O. Box 6651, Baulkham Hills, Business Centre, NSW 2153, Australia

Sterling ISBN 0-8069-9517-3 Trade
                0-8069-9520-3 Paper

to
Caroline

Contents

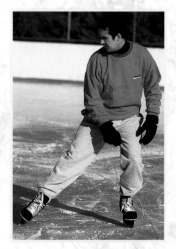

Introduction

*A*fter working as a professional skater and instructor for several years, I am very excited about writing a skating book. Nothing makes me happier than seeing people learn to skate successfully and happily. The great sense of accomplishment and pride from learning a new skill or even just stepping onto the ice for the first time is evident in young and old skaters alike. I am very proud to have worked alongside many great skating coaches and with many wonderful students. As a skating instructor I have reevaluated and tested methods over and over in order to achieve my goal of teaching a particular skill in the clearest, most efficient and successful way. The methods and descriptions in this book have been rigorously tested and have helped countless skaters

improve upon and master skills. I hope you have a similar success with them!

This book is intended as much for persons who want to learn to skate from step one as it is for others who have been skating for several years and who want to master backward crossovers or add power to their stop. It is also intended as a guide for parents who want to teach their children to skate or who plan to enroll them

in skating lessons. Last, I hope other instructors find this a helpful reference that adds to their repertoire of ideas and lessons.

The skills and maneuvers in this book are presented starting with those that most skaters find easy and progressing to those that are considered more difficult. The skills build upon themselves. It would be hard to accomplish a move in chapter 10 if you were not comfortable with the skills in chapters 7 and 8. The terminology builds

on itself as well, so experienced skaters may have to brush up on earlier material to understand the description of certain steps.

If you plan to teach a child to skate, chapter 6 is a guide to explaining the skills and maneuvers to children. Skating is the same, technically, for children and adults, but how it is explained and taught differs greatly. To teach children, you must first understand the skills as they are described to adults and then teach them in a manner most suited to children.

Let me encourage everyone, regardless of age or past athletic experience, to take up skating. It's not that hard—especially with proper instruction! It's great to get started skating as a child, but if you didn't, please don't rule it out as an adult. Throughout North America and Europe are numerous adult *ice hockey leagues, speed skating clubs, figure skating clubs, and recreational skating activities open to people who started skating as adults!*

Finally, with the debut of women's ice hockey in the 1998 Olympics, I particularly encourage women and girls interested in hockey to get hockey skates and consider it an option.

Happy skating!

Aaron Foeste

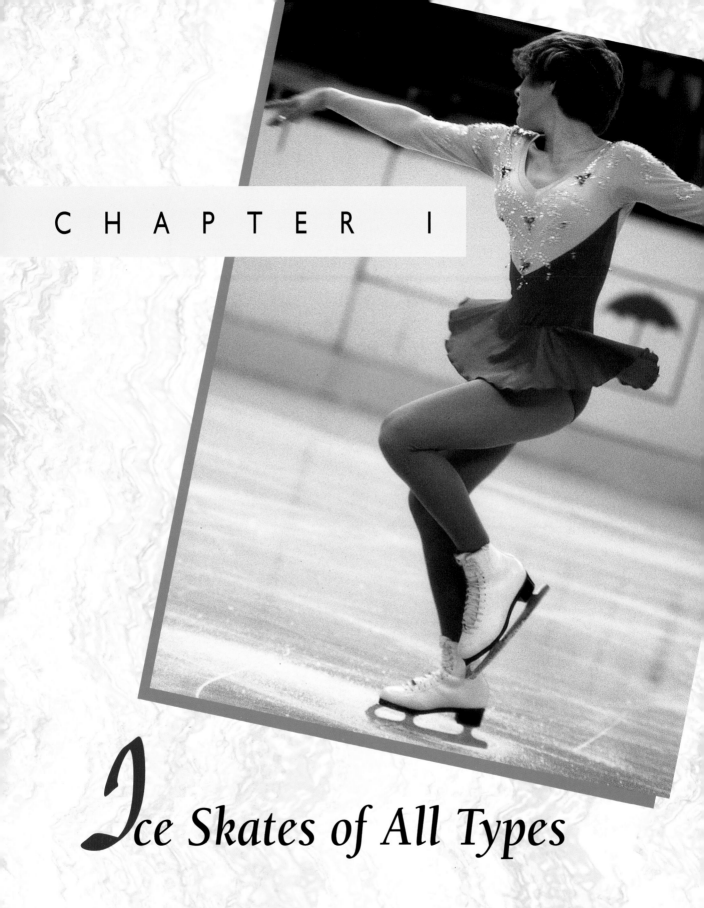

CHAPTER I

Ice Skates of All Types

*n*o one can pinpoint the exact moment in history when someone came up with the idea of strapping bones or antlers onto their feet to make it easier to travel across an expanse of ice. But historical records show that northern Europeans have been skating at least since the 1300s. It's amazing that the basic design of the ice blade hasn't really changed at all!

Rather, ice skate design has undergone refinements as technology has allowed sturdier construction of boots and blades. As modern engineering and refrigeration technology have made it possible for ice to be manufactured anywhere, skating no longer remains the exclusive domain of regions with colder winter weather.

Since the late 19th century, constant improvements in skating equipment and more consistent ice-making methods have enabled skaters to experiment more safely. This has made possible the development of the ice sports that we enjoy today: ice hockey, figure skating, speed skating—and the different styles of skates associated with each sport.

Figure skate

Types of Skates

The Figure Skate
Well-made figure skates are constructed of leather, have a thickly padded tongue, give plenty of ankle support, and have a stainless steel blade screwed onto the boot. The heel lift enhances balance and posture. Note the "pick" that is built into the toe of the blade. The pick is unique to figure skates and is used for jumps and other advanced maneuvers (not for stopping or pushing off!).

Hockey skate

The Speed Skate

In this photo you see a typical speed skate with its characteristic long blade. A speed skating boot is made with a low cuff and is not designed for ankle support, but for ankle flexibility. The upper part of the boot should be made of leather and the bottom of fiberglass or a similar material. The blade and its support are bolted to the bottom of the boot and can be easily removed by the skater.

The Hockey Skate

This photo shows a typical hockey skate. A good hockey skate is made of leather on the inside and is covered with a durable, tear-resistant exterior. A hockey skate should have a hard-plastic toe for protection, a stainless steel blade held in place by a lightweight plastic support, and plenty of ankle support.

Which Type of Skate Should I Rent or Buy?

Beginning and intermediate skaters should not use speed skates, which are highly specialized for their sport. The long blades can be dangerous to novice skaters and the skate does not provide enough support for learning comfortably. If you are interested in speed skating, first spend a season becoming proficient on either hockey or figure skates.

Selecting between figure or hockey skates can pose a dilemma for the beginning skater. Fortunately, the skating motion and all but the most advanced maneuvers are the same on both figure and hockey skates. If you or your child are a fan of one of the two sports or are interested in participating in it, go ahead and start in that particular type of skate. Learning in one type of skate will not pre-

Speed skate

vent you from skating just as well in the other. However, each type has different attributes that may make it more suitable for certain individuals to learn in.

Note the greater area of contact with the surface in the figure skate blade.

The photo shows that the figure skate blade is much longer and has a greater area of contact with the ice than the hockey skate blade. The figure skate blade also extends farther behind the skate than the hockey blade. This can lessen the chance of falling over backward and is a great reason to start small children in figure skates. The small area of contact between the blade of the hockey skate and the ice makes it easy for the skater to make quick starts and stops and sharp turns, but provides slightly less stability for the beginner skater than the figure skate.

If you do not have strong feelings about either hockey or figure skating and are trying to decide which type of skate to use, ask yourself the following questions:

1. Are you an active in-line skater? Hockey skates will feel more like your in-line skates. Because you can already skate, make sure you work on your ice skating stop immediately, as it is not the same as stopping on in-line skates.

2. Are you an active skier? With their heel lift and longer blade, figure skates will help you gain the correct sense of skating balance and help eliminate any "leaning back" from skiing more quickly than hockey skates.

3. Are you nervous or apprehensive about learning to skate or about trying to learn new physical skills? The long blade and raised heel of the figure skate will give you better posture and balance than a hockey skate.

4. Are you extremely tall or heavy? Again, figure skates will provide better balance.

5. Do you plan to only skate a few times a season? Using figure skates will make it easier to regain a sense of balance after having time off between skating sessions.

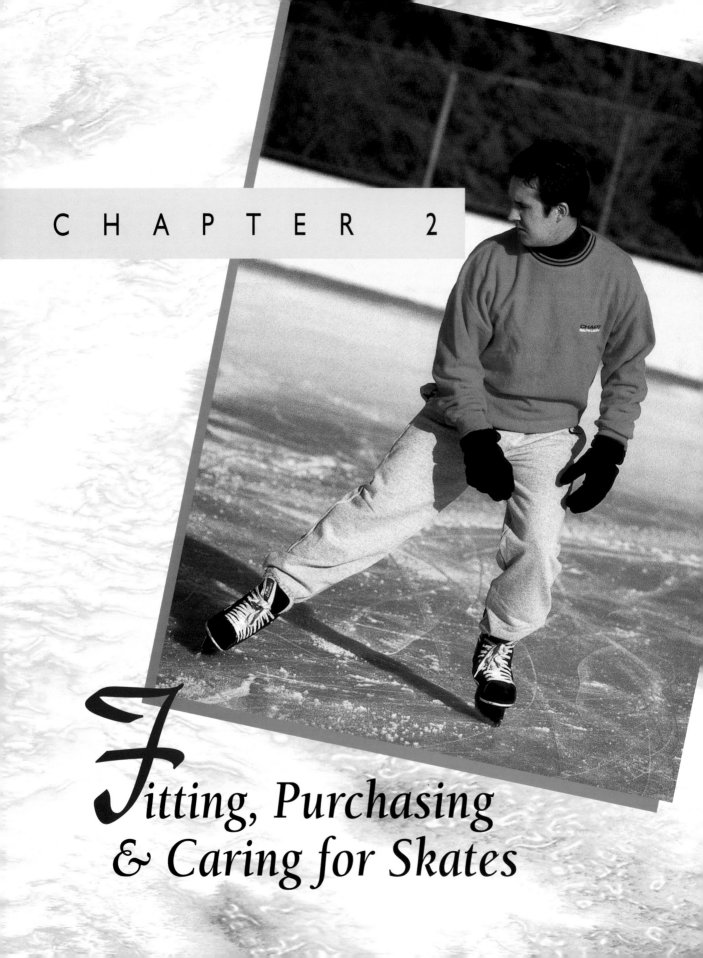

CHAPTER 2

Fitting, Purchasing
& Caring for Skates

a properly fitted and maintained skate is crucial to enjoying skating and learning to skate successfully. When you skate, your blades remain flat against the ice and do not roll from heel to toe as your feet do when you run or walk. Because the foot has no heel-to-toe rocking motion, it isn't necessary to allow for flexibility and extra room at the toe of the skate as you would in a properly fitted shoe. In fact, in a skate that fits well, your toes should just be able to touch the end of the skate boot—an "exact" match to your foot.

Socks

Getting a proper fit in a skate starts with wearing the proper socks. Socks should not add any significant bulk to your foot; skates should not be sized to allow for several pairs of thick socks. Thin cotton or synthetic sports socks are ideal. If blisters or chafing becomes a problem, try

Try putting a make-up pad over any blisters or pressure points.

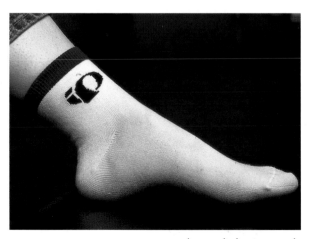

A good skating sock

two very thin pairs of socks: the socks will rub against each other instead of rubbing against your foot. Even if you will be skating outdoors in cold weather, stick with thin socks, not bulky wool ones, and use layers for warmth. Thick socks will make it more difficult to control your skates, your feet will move around inside the boots, and you may get blisters!

Quality of the Skate

Before trying on a new or used skate, make sure it has the proper ankle support for skating. Squeeze the back of the boot by the ankle. There should be very little movement of the boot. If you can squeeze the sides of the boot together, it is a poor-quality product or is broken down and you should not consider it.

The ankle of a skate with the proper support is very difficult to squeeze together.

Skate Fitting

Don't be surprised if your skate size is smaller than your shoe size. When rent-

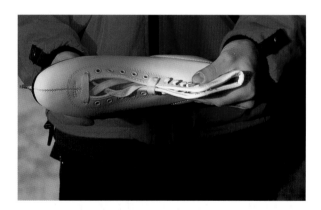

Don't buy this skate; it has no ankle support!

ing or buying skates, start with one size lower than your shoes and keep trying skates in half-size increments until you find the best fit. Always seek the advice of an experienced salesperson at a well-respected skate shop, but beware of advice from employees at large department stores or sporting goods chains that have only a small skate section.

Follow these steps to find a skate that fits well:

1. Loosen the laces significantly three-quarters of the way down the boot in order to slip your foot in or out of a skate. Don't spend time pushing, pulling, or prying your foot into or out of a boot that is only loosened at the top.

2. With your foot in the boot, bang your heel lightly on the floor to get your heel all the way to the back of the boot.

3. Beginning with the lower laces, pull all the laces snugly until you reach the top

eyelet of the skate and tie the laces firmly, but not tightly. Your ankles should feel comfortable.

4. Stand up and do some deep knee bends. You should be able to wiggle your toes. Your toes should be able to touch the end of the skate lightly but should not be cramped or bent in any way. The bottom of your foot should not be able to slide or rock from side to side inside of the boot.

5. If the skates seem to fit well, keep them on for 5 to 10 minutes and continue to stand or walk around the store. This will help you identify any pressure points or discomfort. Do not purchase uncomfortable skates.

The hard toes on most skates make it impossible to use your hand to feel how close your toes, or your child's, are to the end of the boot. Some skates, particularly hockey skates, have a removable foot bed. Place it on the floor and stand on it to see how your foot measures up to the size of

You can use the foot-bed from the skate to check for size.

the skate. If you are purchasing a child's skate you can also compare a shoe to the skate. The skate should appear to be the same size as the shoe or slightly smaller than it. Don't purchase skates with enough room for your child to "grow into" them. Skates sized like this will make skating very difficult until the child does, in fact, "grow into" them.

Used Skates

The ideal way for parents to keep their children in properly fitted skates—which may be outgrown each season—and to keep costs low, is to buy and sell used skates. Used skates are a great way for adults to find a bargain as well. High-quality used skates are just as good as new ones and have already undergone the sometimes bothersome "breaking in" process. You should check for support

and you should fit a used skate the same way you would a new one. In addition, follow these guidelines when purchasing used skates:

1. Don't buy skates that smell bad.

2. Check the blade to make sure it is straight and not warped or bent.

3. Make sure the blade has not been sharpened down too close to the support (as it has in the skate on the right of the picture below).

4. Don't buy skates with holes or tears in the inside or outside.

5. Used skates should be, at most, half the current price of the new skate, except with slightly used, top-of-the-line skates, which should be 25% to 50% less than the new price.

on the ice can help save the edges of your blades from becoming dull too quickly. Guards are available in different models, can be adjusted for almost all skate sizes, and come in a variety of colors. Please remember to take off your skate guards before stepping onto the ice! This will save you from some rather embarrassing, and possibly painful, moments!

Most skaters put "soakers" over their blades to store them after they have wiped them off. Soakers are usually made of terry cloth and absorb any moisture that may have been left on the blade or that forms from condensation.

Skate Care

Whenever you come off the ice for the day, remember to wipe off your skate blades. Even though they are made of stainless steel, they can still rust if moisture is left on them.

Skate guards are available for both figure and hockey skates. Wearing these guards to walk around when you are not

A hard plastic skate guard

Wipe blades dry after each use.

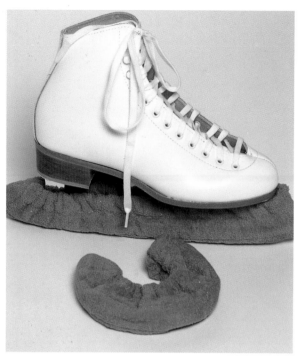

A soft, absorbent skate guard

Blade Sharpening

Skate blades have to be sharpened regularly. The bottom of a skate blade is not meant to be flat. Rather, it has two edges, and the bottom of the blade should resemble a shallow "V". As you will learn, you need these two edges in order to start, stop, and turn on your skates. The average recreational skater should have his or her skates sharpened after every 10 to15 sessions on the ice.

New skates are always sold unsharpened, but most good skate shops will sharpen a new pair of skates for you free when you make your purchase. Don't leave the shop without having your skates

sharpened! Don't let the sharpener give you the deepest "V" cut available. Ask for a shallow sharpening. This will give you enough edge to skate effectively, and will also enable you to get used to sliding on your skates when your are learning how to stop.

A skate blade that is too sharp can actually be dangerous! You must have a certain amount of strength and skill in order to control very sharp skates. A sharp skate blade causes most beginners to stop too quickly and puts you at risk of spraining an ankle.

A skate blade that is too dull can also be dangerous! If you find your feet slipping out from under you to the sides, you need to have the skates sharpened. When renting skates, always return dull skates and insist on a sharp pair.

A skate being sharpened

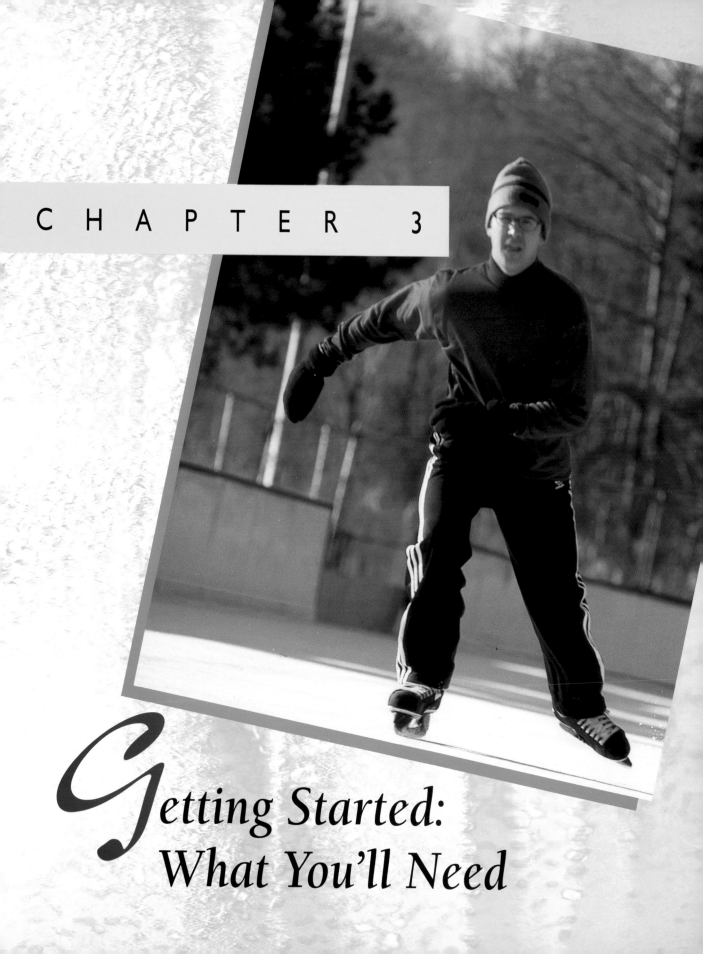

CHAPTER 3

Getting Started:
What You'll Need

*U*sing the proper clothing and equipment will add greatly to your skating enjoyment. Weather conditions can vary from bright sun and a wind chill factor in the negative numbers at a pond in January, to humid, pleasantly cool conditions at an indoor rink in May. Keep in mind that you'll be producing heat and be perspiring as you skate. Consider wearing protective gear, which can be worn underneath regular clothing. Use the following tips to choose clothing and gear for your activity and for planning your first day at the rink.

Clothing

You can wear almost anything you want when you go ice skating, but you should consider the following:

1. Some indoor rinks are much colder than others. You may need only a sweatshirt on top at one rink, and a down coat at another.

2. Always wear gloves or mittens when you skate. You'll need to put your hands on the ice to get up after a fall.

3. Dress in layers so that you can add or remove clothing as you need it.

4. Don't wear tight-fitting pants or long skirts or dresses. All will hinder proper leg movement and may lead to falls.

5. Don't tuck your pants into your skates. This can cause chafing or blisters around the ankle.

6. The ice magnifies sun glare; take sunglasses along when you skate outdoors.

Helmets are a good idea for young skaters.

Protective Gear

Consider a bicycle or hockey helmet for yourself or your child. Helmets can often be rented at the skate-rental counter. Also, in-line skating pads—wrist guards, knee pads, and elbow pads—can be worn

Pads can be worn over or under clothing.

Lessons and Classes

Even for experienced athletes, a lesson or class is a great way to get started in ice skating. Under the watchful eye of a professional skater and skilled teacher, you can save time learning how to move and stop. Many new skaters find it helpful to take lessons, and group lessons can be a good way to meet people and learn to skate in the company of other beginners.

Lessons and classes are especially important for young beginners. I have seen children cry hysterically and not want to step on the ice while exasperated parents try to prod them into action. Often a lesson with other children away from parents will get a youngster focused on skating, playing games, and having fun on the ice. Pros usually work with children daily and have a variety of games and incentives to offer the reluctant child.

over or under your clothing while ice skating. If you are very worried about injury, padded pants used by figure skaters and stunt skaters can also be worn under loose-fitting pants or sweat pants. The best way to avoid an accident, however, is to take a lesson from a pro and make sure your skates are properly fitted and maintained.

Teaching Children: Fun at the Rink

If you decide to teach your child yourself, make sure to read both Chapter 6, "Teaching a Child to Skate," and the other chapters that describe the technical aspects of skating. The most important thing to remember in teaching a child to skate is this: let the child have fun! Children who have fun at the rink will

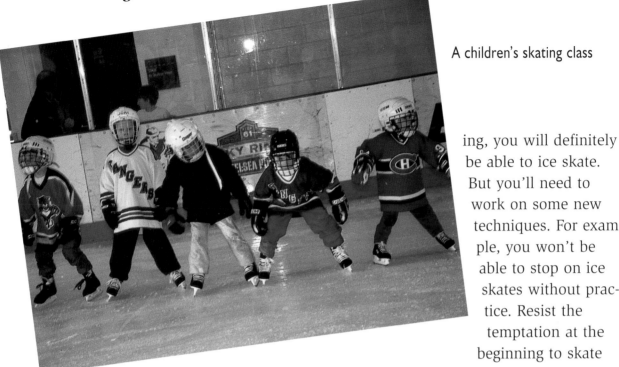

A children's skating class

ing, you will definitely be able to ice skate. But you'll need to work on some new techniques. For example, you won't be able to stop on ice skates without practice. Resist the temptation at the beginning to skate around the rink fast. Instead, spend much of the first half hour on ice skates working on the stop (see Chapter 5). It will also take some time to build confidence and balance on ice skates, which will feel slightly less stable, because in-line skates have relatively wide wheels and a long wheel base.

want to return and are more likely to go onto the ice and try new things. You don't want your child to associate the skating rink with fear or overbearing parents. Don't worry if your child doesn't learn to stop or turn (or even skate) right away! As long as he or she has fun, the first day should be considered a success.

A Note to In-Line Skaters

If in-line skates are like four-wheel-drive trucks, ice skates are like sports cars. The skating motion and most of the maneuvers of in-line skating are the same in ice skating—everything just happens much faster and with much more precision on ice skates! If you can handle in-line skat-

Call Ahead

Call your local skating rink before going to a public skating session. Find out the times that are good for beginners and when beginner classes or lessons are available. That way, you can avoid finding yourself at the rink on disco night or during a school field trip your first time on skates.

CHAPTER 4

The Adult Beginner

*f*or those of you who have spent time in-line skating, snow skiing, or participating in other sports that require focus and concentration on balance, ice skating will be a nice addition to your skills.

But if you're a new skater who hasn't had this kind of experience, you may feel a little hesitant about stepping onto the ice for the first time. You may be concerned about falling and hurting yourself. However, with a little preparation and guidance accidents are rare. Just give yourself a few sessions to get the hang of it and don't be too critical of yourself. It's hard to keep in mind when you see them gliding gracefully across the ice, but the world's great skaters were all initially a little wobbly (and fell once or twice!).

Off-Ice Warm-Ups

Many beginners like to get the feel of balancing on their skates before trying to balance on the ice. Feel free to walk around at home in your skates—with the proper skate guards on! Many skaters find that this helps with the break-in process with

new skates as well. If you're a new skater, make sure to spend a few minutes walking around in the skates on the rubberized surface adjacent the rink before stepping onto the ice. Do some knee bends and practice shifting your weight from side to side. Also make sure to review mentally what to do if you lose your balance or feel as if you're going to fall.

Keeping Your Balance

The natural response to feeling like you're going to fall is to stand up straighter to avoid hitting the ground (or the ice!). This is the worst thing to do on ice skates and is sure to make you fall every time you do it! Train yourself to bend at the knees and waist and to touch your knees or toes when you feel off balance. This will lower your center of gravity and help you regain balance.

1. Here instructor Cam Millar demonstrates being off balance by keeping his center of gravity too high and too far back.

2. He has fully regained balance by bending forward and touching his knees...

3. ...and can now return to a normal skating position.

Onto the Ice!

Immediately hold on to the wall after stepping on the ice for the first time. Do some knee bends, shift your weight from side to side and try lifting one foot and then the other if you can. If you can balance and move about, try as soon as possible to avoid relying on the wall. Many new skaters are hindered by the need to keep a hand on the wall, and more accidents occur from falling into the wall than on open ice.

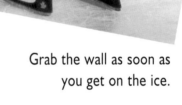

Grab the wall as soon as
you get on the ice.

Practice shifting your weight
and doing knee bends.

Proper position for a knee bend: head and chest forward, knees bent, and shins pressed into the tongues of the skates

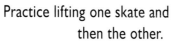
Practice lifting one skate and then the other.

The Fall

It's going to happen—and most new skaters are very happy to learn that falling and getting back up aren't so bad if you remember to follow a few important steps! Also, make sure to get up quickly after you fall so other skaters don't hit you or skate into you.

1. Try to regain balance by touching your toes (or knees) and do a deep knee bend.

2. Make sure you have your balance...

3. ...and slowly stand up.

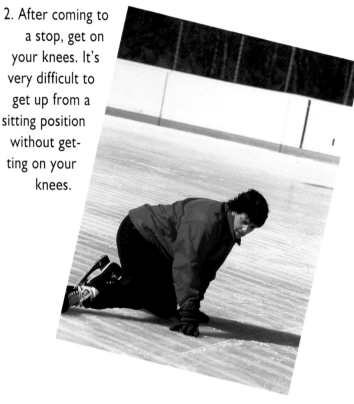

2. After coming to a stop, get on your knees. It's very difficult to get up from a sitting position without getting on your knees.

1. When you fall, tuck your chin to your chest (to avoid hitting the back of your head on the ice) and continue to bend as low as possible until you gently roll or fall onto your butt.

3. Keep your hands down for balance and bring one knee up until your skate is back on the ice. Then, bring the other skate up. Remember to get up quickly so you're not in other skaters' way—and so you don't get wet.

Moving Forward: The Duck Walk

This exercise is skating—that is, it teaches you how to move forward on skates and evolves naturally into the skating stride. The name "duck walk" probably originated in children's skating classes and most accurately describes the "toes pointed out, waddling motion" of the process. If you do not turn your toes out like a duck (or a dancer), the edges of your blades will have nothing to push against and your first attempt at moving will look more like running on a treadmill and you'll go nowhere.

The following photos show the duck walk. Start with your knees bent, your hands on your knees or thighs for stability, and your toes turned out. Slowly step forward a few inches with one foot and then step forward with the other while maintaining the toes-out position. As you step farther forward you will begin to develop a stride. Try to let yourself glide a little after each step.

1

2

3

4

5

Gliding

After picking up a little speed doing the duck walk, place both skates on the ice, toes forward (parallel), and glide (keep your hands on your knees for balance). After gliding, resume the duck walk and practice the glide again after every five to ten steps.

Gliding on two feet

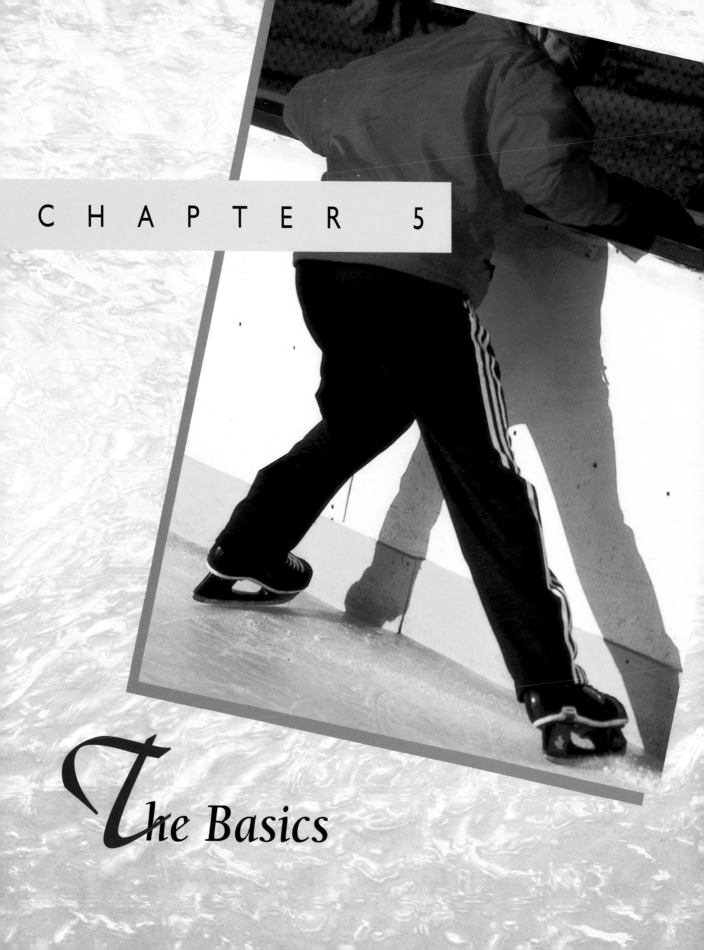

CHAPTER 5

The Basics

*n*ow that you're comfortable on the ice and can move about, it's time to work on the fundamentals of skating. This chapter concentrates on basic stopping, turning, and the swizzle—a power-skating exercise that is vital to all intermediate and advanced skating maneuvers.

It will become obvious to you very quickly when you do these exercises that the edges of your skate blades and how you push against them are very important! Look at the definitions in the box at right to understand what I am referring to when I describe an exercise. If you take skating lessons, you are sure to hear the instructor mention these.

As you develop your skating technique it is important to keep two things in mind: First of all, good skaters can do everything in either direction. Make sure to practice everything with both feet and do all turns in both directions. And second, if you are wearing figure skates, do not use your toe pick for stopping or propulsion. The toe pick is for advanced jumps only. You will not progress very far as a skater if you use it for other purposes.

Inside Edge
the side of the skate blade that faces the other skate

Outside Edge
the side of the skate blade that faces away from the other skate

Inside Leg
when skating in a circle, the leg closest to the center of the circle

Outside Leg
when skating in a circle, the leg farthest from the center of the circle

Stopping

The first stop skaters learn is the snow-plow stop. If you are familiar with skiing, you are no doubt very familiar with the idea of doing the "snowplow" on the ski slope. Doing a snowplow on ice skates is virtually identical to doing a skier's snow-plow. Learning the snowplow is the key to moving on to the impressive "hockey stop." Don't be surprised if it takes you a few sessions of skating to feel really com-fortable with your stop. You should devote the majority of your first hours on skates to learning how to stop: once a new skater can stop, he or she is much more comfortable and confident about trying new exercises.

Learning to slide your skate sideways across the ice is crucial to stopping. Practice this by holding the wall and pushing one foot to the side like the skater in the following pictures. Push with your inside edge against the ice. Your blade should scrape a fine layer of ice from the surface with each push, and you should be left with a small pile of snow at the end of your skate!

1. Hold the wall...

2. ...and push against the inside edge of your skate until you've made a small pile of snow!

1. Make sure you practice pushing with both the left and the right skates.

2. Making snow!

Snowplow Stop— One Foot

Once you're comfortable pushing your skate sideways while holding on to the wall, it's time to try the same thing while moving: a snowplow stop with one foot.

1. Start moving and come to a glide with both hands on one knee (instead of the wall!) for support...

Snowplow Stop—Two Feet

1. Start moving and come to a glide with your hands on each knee for support...

2. ...and push your skate to the side just like you did while holding the wall. This should bring you to a stop.

2. ...and push to the side across the ice with both feet: a snowplow stop with two feet. Note how the toes are turned slightly toward each other.

Basic Turns

You are now about to discover how important the positioning of your upper body is while skating! By turning your head, chest, and shoulders in the direction you wish to go, you will be able to cause yourself to turn with very little extra effort. Developing the proper upper body positioning is critical to making smooth turns. The same positioning used in this basic turn will be needed in all intermediate and advanced turns. Make sure to practice left and right turns equally!

1. Start moving and come to a glide with both feet a little wider than shoulder width. Both skates should be on their inside edges.

2. Turn your head, chest, and shoulders in the direction you wish to turn while maintaining the position of your feet.

3. Continue to keep your head, chest, and shoulders turned as you make the turn. You should also be pushing against the inside edge of your outside skate now.

4. Notice how my shoulders are parallel to the ice and not dipped like an airplane! This is the proper position for turning.

5. Continue to maintain the upper body position and pressure against the inside edge of the outside skate until you have completed your turn.

Swizzles

The skating motions involved in the swizzle can be found in just about any skating maneuver. Mastering swizzles will make learning everything else on skates—including skating backward—much easier! Swizzles will also develop important "skating muscles" in your thighs, inner thighs, groin, and butt.

While doing swizzles you will propel yourself forward without ever lifting a skate off the ice. Shifting your weight and pushing with your edges will be used to accomplish this. It is very important to distinguish the sideways push you did (to come to a stop) from the push involved in swizzles. The only time your skate should ever slide sideways against the ice is during a stop. In swizzles, you push to the side but your inside edges dig into the ice and the force propels you forward. There are three component steps to a swizzle: the bend, the push, and the recovery. Take a look at the following photos.

1. Begin with your feet together and your toes pointed out (hands on thighs for stability).

2. Do a deep knee bend and begin to push out with your skates.

3. Push out with both skates. This will propel you forward powerfully.

4. After the push, turn your toes toward each other and begin to bring your legs together and return to the starting position. This is called the recovery.

5. Begin the entire process again now. You should have moved forward several feet during the swizzle. See if you can go from one end of the rink to the other doing nothing but swizzles!

CHAPTER 6

Teaching a Child to Skate

One of the most enjoyable aspects of teaching children is seeing the look on their faces when they realize they have "discovered" a new and miraculous sense of balance and self-confidence on ice skates! It's so different from walking! It's no wonder children's eyes open wide with wonder when they see ice skaters for the first time. Skating is awfully strange when you think about it, but it can be made to seem as natural as walking. Children prove this all the time!

Chapter 3 discussed skating classes and private lessons. This chapter is for people who are comfortable on skates and want to teach a child to skate or who want to learn to skate along with a child. If both you and the child are learning together and you find it difficult to skate—and, therefore, difficult to help the child—you should put the child (and yourself!) in a skating class.

The skating maneuvers and exercises discussed in the previous two chapters and in the following chapters are exactly the same for children and adults: it is how this information is conveyed to children that is different. Rely on those chapters for the technical information needed to learn and perform the different skating moves, and use this chapter for help in teaching the techniques to children. As you incorporate the games, contests, and methods from this chapter into your day at the rink, let your imagination go. Come up with your own creative ways to help a child learn the fundamentals of skating. Of course, understanding the fundamentals yourself will help you accomplish this goal.

A successful day at the rink is one in which a child has fun! Your lesson plan must be very flexible and filled with fun and games. Children under seven years old should never be expected to concentrate on a lesson that lasts more than 15 to 30 minutes. Also, please don't underestimate the value of simply skating around the rink or chasing friends. This is very valuable time on skates for developing ankle strength and balance. Often children will turn, skate, or stop more naturally while playing than when they are concentrating on skating.

Finally, always do the exercises with the child. You will be a friend who is skating and playing, rather than a teacher.

Getting Ready for the Ice

Let your child walk around on skates outside the ice surface for a few minutes to get used to the skates. Children find it exciting to watch other skaters before going onto the ice themselves if it is their first time at the rink. When it's time to go on the ice, explain to them that they will need to bend and touch their knees or toes if they feel off balance (see page 41). Have them practice a few times, and let them practice falling and getting back up if they want to! Tell them to keep their hands on their knees for the first couple of minutes that they are on the ice.

Holding
a child from behind

Holding a Child While on the Ice

Don't offer to hold a child's hand! It's better that children not know this option is available. They will learn to skate much faster on their own. If your child asks to hold your hand, suggest that he put his hands on his knees instead. Encourage the child to try skating alone. If the child persists, go ahead. It's better for you to hold on to a new skater's wrist than for the skater to hold on to you. Holding hands does not give you much stabilizing power, especially when you are trying to hold very small hands. It is easier to hold some children under their arms from behind. Keep your skates about shoulder width apart, and the child's skates should fit comfortably between yours. This is a great way to give a child a ride on the ice! At no time should you or anyone else—no matter how skilled—pick up a child and, while skating, carry him. A child carried this way could be seriously hurt in a fall.

Falling and Getting Back Up

For your sake and your child's, children should learn to get up unassisted after falling. Children are not afraid to fall and will do so frequently. To avoid being injured or causing injury to other skaters, it is very important not to lie down on the ice after a fall. The best way to teach a child to stand up after a fall is to get down on the ice and demonstrate. This also prevents the child from asking to be picked up! Only help a child get up after he has made a few unsuccessful attempts alone.

1. Demonstrate how to bend and touch your toes to regain balance—or tuck your chin to your chest and fall onto your butt from this position.

2. After the first fall, get down on the ice with the child.

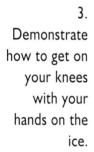

3. Demonstrate how to get on your knees with your hands on the ice.

4. Keep your hands on the ice and bring your feet up underneath you.

5. Stand up...

6. ...and make sure you have your balance.

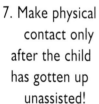

7. Make physical contact only after the child has gotten up unassisted!

Moving—The Duck Walk *(from Chapter 4)*

Have your child keep his hands on his knees and his toes pointed outward and walk like a duck. Good instructors have children moving around the rink quacking like ducks in a matter of minutes! Walking like this evolves quickly and naturally into a skating stride once the child is comfortable. You don't even need to teach the stride, just encourage the child to glide between "duck" steps. Move several feet ahead of your child. Encourage the child to skate to you.

Practice lifting a skate off the ice.

Getting Ready to Move

Help your child overcome the fear of lifting a skate off the ice (necessary in order to move!). Practice marching in place, hands on knees for support. Have a balancing contest to see who can keep a skate off the ice the longest! (Your sense of humor is very important to a child's learning process!)

Pushing a Chair or Cone

For a small child who has trouble balancing or moving forward, holding on to a cone or chair and pushing it is a great way to learn to skate. It is analogous to using training wheels on a bicycle and can make the difference between leaving the rink after five minutes or staying all day. Many rinks make cones or chairs available to small children, but make sure you get permission before having your child skate this way.

Pushing a cone is a great way for a small child to learn to skate.

Basic Turning
(*from Chapter 5*)

Children don't want to hear about inside edges and upper-body positions. They want to know that turning is magic: You'll always go in the direction you turn and look!

Stopping *(from Chapter 5)*

Have your child practice the same steps an adult would. Emphasize "making snow." Children love to see their blades scrape snow off the ice as they learn to stop. Point out the snow and the tracks that are left on the ice after they try to stop. Have snow-making contests (but don't pick up the snow—a rule at most rinks!).

Gliding

Gliding on one or both skates is very important in developing a good stride and in learning other skating moves. Have contests to see how far your child can glide without moving his feet after picking up speed.

Swizzles *(from Chapter 5)*

Have your child try to make it around the rink without lifting a skate off the ice by doing swizzles. Many children think the motion of a swizzle looks like a swimming frog, and they like to pretend they're frogs when they do swizzles.

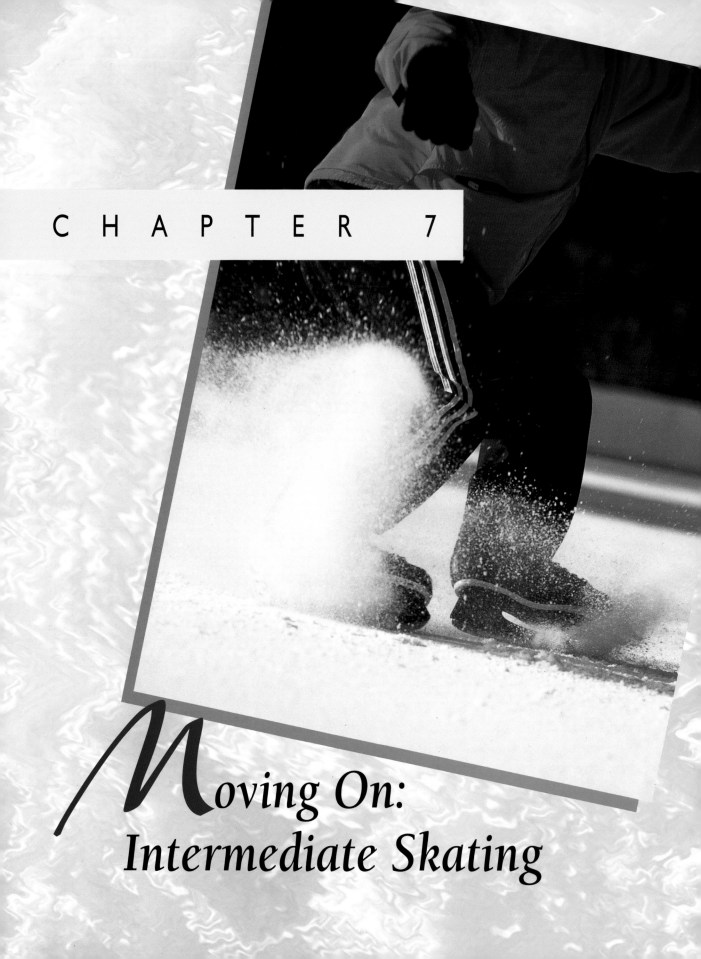

CHAPTER 7

*M*oving On:
Intermediate Skating

*t*he maneuvers in this chapter accomplish the same thing as their more basic counterparts: they make you stop or turn. However, the more advanced maneuvers are much more efficient and more effective at higher speeds (and, hopefully, more fun!). As you might expect, more skill will be needed to do the hockey stop or outside-edge turn. These moves require balancing on the outside edge of one of your skates—which takes more balance. Master the basic turn or stop before advancing to the next level, so that you will find it much easier to learn these more challenging moves.

The Hockey Stop!

Here's what you've all been waiting for: the hockey stop! Figure skaters do exactly the same stop as hockey players, but the name "hockey stop" has always been used to refer to this stop. Again, figure skaters do not use their toe picks to stop!

The hockey stop is the most powerful stop available to skaters. The stop can bring a skater moving at top speed to a complete stop in a few feet. It is quite spectacular, because the skate blades shoot ice chips and snow into the air as they dig into the ice. Learn to do the hockey stop while skating slowly at first (and you won't spray very much snow into the air), so you can practice the timing and develop the necessary ankle strength. When you turn sideways into the stop, your blades should maintain contact with the ice—don't jump into the stopping position.

I. Get moving (slowly at first!).

2. Turn your hips and skates perpendicular to the direction you were moving (keep your upper body facing the direction you were skating) and bend your knees. Slide your blades sideways against the ice. The forward skate should be on its inside edge, the back skate on its outside edge.

3. Dig in! Keep pushing down through your edges as you slide across the ice.

4. Notice how both skates are spraying snow. It takes a lot of strength to keep your back skate down and on its outside edge during this stop. I've purposely kept my back foot a little forward for the photo to show this. When you're learning the hockey stop, simply keep the back skate on the ice and don't worry if it's not digging in right away.

5. Snow really flies during a quick hockey stop!

6. Less than a second later...

7. ...completely stopped in just a few feet.

The Outside-Edge Turn

Whenever you make a turn on skates you must turn your head, chest, and shoulders in the direction you want to turn. Developing good form in your basic turn will help you with this turn and with crossovers in the future. You might hear the outside-edge turn called the "airplane turn." Make sure you don't dip one shoulder like an airplane, though. This turn can be done at high speeds, and is much sharper and quicker than the basic turn.

To execute the outside-edge turn, come to a glide and slide your inside skate forward—it's going to lead the way around the turn. Now turn your upper body into the turn. Your inside skate, which is leading, should be on the outside edge and your trailing skate on the inside edge.

You'll find the hockey stop and the outside-edge turn easier to accomplish in one direction than the other. Don't favor one side—make sure you practice both directions equally!

1. Start moving...

2. ...and slide your inside skate forward.

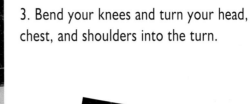

3. Bend your knees and turn your head, chest, and shoulders into the turn.

4. Maintain your upper body positioning throughout the turn.

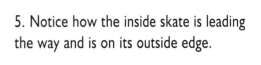

5. Notice how the inside skate is leading the way and is on its outside edge.

6. Notice how the outside skate is on its inside edge.

7. Knees should be bent slightly, and more than half of your weight should be on the front (inside) leg.

8. Start to face forward...

9. ...and come out of the turn by turning your head, chest, and shoulders straight ahead.

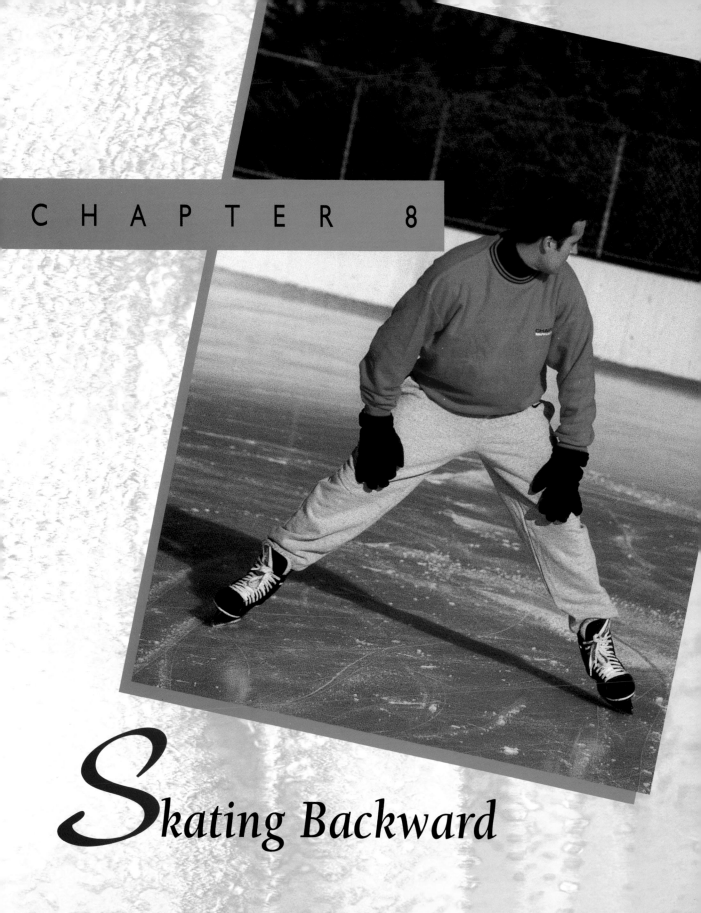

CHAPTER 8

Skating Backward

Skating backward is not that hard! In fact, if you can do swizzles, you can skate backward—or more precisely, you can do backward swizzles. Once you're comfortable with a few basic forward maneuvers, you should begin to work some backward skating exercises into your repertoire. If you feel off balance while moving backward, bend forward and touch your knees or toes just as you would when skating forward. Also, make sure to look behind you as you skate.

Backward Swizzles

If you can do forward swizzles, try backward swizzles. The steps are exactly the same: bend, push, and recover. To get warmed up, do one forward swizzle and finish with your toes pointed at one another (heels pointed out). Now repeat the same three steps you did in your first swizzle, except do them backward: do a deep knee bend with your toes pointed in, push out with your legs so you move backward, and recover by bringing your heels together and standing up straighter. Try rocking back and forth, doing one forward swizzle followed by one backward swizzle. Your skates should move back and forth in a pattern that resembles an oval. This will get you accustomed to the backward motion, and is good practice for stopping while skating backward.

1. Start with your toes together and heels pointed out (hands on knees for stability).

2. Do a deep knee bend and start to push out
with the inside edges of your skates.

3. Push all the way out with your inside edges.
You should be moving backward at this point.

4. Turn your heels toward each other, start to
stand up, and bring your legs together. You should
be fully recovered, gliding backward, and ready to
start the process again!

Backward Swizzles—One Leg at a Time

Backward swizzles can be done with one leg at a time (so can forward swizzles!), using the same steps. During backward swizzles, like forward ones, your skates never leave the ice. In fact, the backward skating motion very closely resembles doing a swizzle with one leg, and then the other, over and over again. Look at the following photos in which I do a swizzle with one leg, and then the other.

1. Put your hands on one knee for support, bend and push with the other leg.

2. Push with your inside edge all the way to the side...

3. ...and begin your recovery by turning your heel back toward your other skate and bringing your legs together.

4. At this point you should be gliding backward.

5. Put your hands on your other knee, turn your heel away from your body and begin to bend and push with the other leg.

6. Push all the way out while remembering to look behind.

7. Now you should be gliding backward even faster!

Stopping

The backward snowplow is exactly the same as the forward snowplow—except your toes will point out (not in) as you push your skates to the side across the ice.

The backward snowplow stop. Keep your hand on your knees for support, and your skates should scrape a fine layer of ice from the surface as you come to a stop.

Basic Turns

Again, the basic backward turn is very similar to the basic turn you learned going forward. You'll need to turn your head, chest, and shoulders in the direction you wish to go and push with the inside edge of the outside skate.

2. Turn your head, chest, and shoulders in the direction you wish to go and push hard with the inside edge of your outside skate.

1. Come to a glide with your feet a little wider than shoulder width. Try putting your hands on the thigh or hip of your inside leg to help center your weight over your inside skate.

3. Maintain your upper body positioning and keep pushing with your outside skate.

4. Almost done...

5. As long as you keep pressure on the outside leg and keep your upper body turned, you'll keep turning.

CHAPTER 9

Awesome Forward Crossovers

*f*orward crossovers are essential for figure skaters, hockey players, and speed skaters. Unlike all other turns—which decrease your speed while changing the direction in which you are moving—crossovers allow you to maintain speed or even accelerate while turning.

The forward crossover can be broken down into steps, and these steps can be practiced as individual skating exercises. Working on these steps before trying to put them together will make it much easier for you to master forward crossovers. The steps to forward crossovers are great skating drills and are great for improving overall balance and strength.

The Scooter

This exercise is a real muscle strengthener. Propel yourself forward using the same motions you would use riding a scooter or a skateboard, pushing with only one skate while gliding on the outside edge of the other.

1. Turn
your head, chest, and shoulders
toward the center of your circle. Your feet
should be close together to maximize the push.

3. At the end of the push, lift the outside skate and return it to the starting position. Glide on the outside edge of your inside skate.

2. Bend at the knees and push only with the outside leg (similar to the push in forward swizzles).

4. Finish with feet close (not wide!) and prepare to start the next push.

Stationary Crossovers

It is very important to practice stationary crossovers before undertaking moving crossovers. While walking sideways on the ice you will practice actually crossing one foot over the other. Always keep your blades perpendicular to your line of travel and try to keep your toes from pointing in the direction you are walking during this exercise. Make sure to practice walking both to the left and to the right.

1. Stand with knees bent and feet about shoulder width apart.

2. Step up and over one foot with the other...

4. Step out
from behind with your back foot...

3. ...and place your foot comfortably on the other side of the foot you stepped over. Note how one skate is now on the outside edge.

5. ...and return to a position with your feet about shoulder width apart.

Forward Crossovers

Now it's time to put the steps together and do crossovers! As in all skating exercises, make sure to practice going to the left as much as going to the right. All new skaters will find it much easier to do crossovers in one direction than the other. Make sure to practice both directions!

2. After completing the push, don't place your outside foot down next to your inside skate—step over it instead!

I.
Turn your head, chest, and shoulders toward the center of the circle and start with a scooter push.

4. Step out from behind with your back foot.

3. Transfer your weight to the skate that has completed the cross.

5. Finish with feet close together and prepare to start the next push!

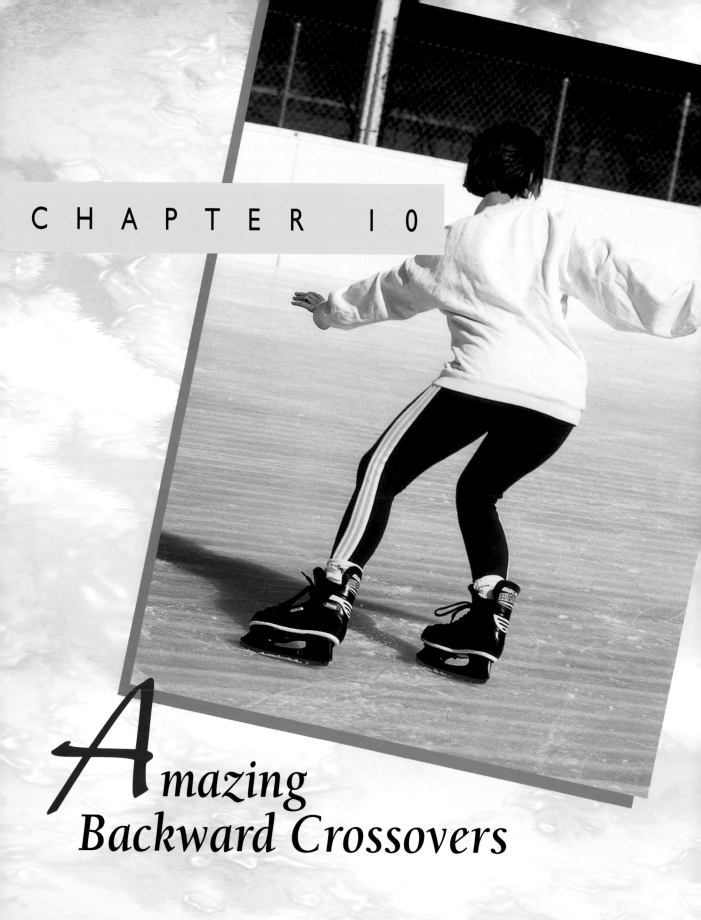

CHAPTER 10

Amazing
Backward Crossovers

*i*f you have ever watched a figure skating competition you have seen skaters making powerful cuts across the ice doing backward crossovers right before launching into a spectacular jump. Backward crossovers are one of the most powerful ways for a skater to pick up speed while skating through a turn. Ice hockey players who play defense can skate backward and cut from side to side using backward crossovers just as quickly as opponents skating forward at them.

Backward crossovers accomplish the same thing as forward crossovers: they maintain a skater's speed (or accelerate him or her) around a circle. However, there are some important technical differences. In forward crossovers the outside foot is stepped over the inside foot, causing the legs to cross, and then the inside leg is stepped out from behind the outside leg to uncross the legs. In backward crossovers the outside skate is not lifted; rather, it remains on the ice as the legs scissor and cross. After crossing, the inside leg is stepped out from behind the outside leg to uncross the legs. The outside skate is never lifted from the ice during backward crossovers!

Walking Backward Around a Circle

This exercise is a great way to get the feel of backward crossovers. March backward, crossing and uncrossing your legs to make a small circle. When you actually do back crossovers while skating, you won't lift your outside skate off the ice, but practicing this way will make it much easier to learn backward crossovers.

Start by imagining a small circle painted on the ice, or pick an object like a cone to walk around, as shown in the photos. As you walk backward around the circle, your steps should consist of either crossing or uncrossing your legs. The most important part of the exercise is to keep your blades at a tangent to the circle, which will require you to rotate your inside hip around the circle as you walk. As you get better at this, try to glide a little each time you uncross your legs. And, as always, remember to practice in both directions!

1. Turn your head, chest, and shoulders toward the center of your circle.

2. Step over your inside skate (toward the center of the circle) with your outside skate.

3. Step out from behind with your inside skate. Remember to rotate your inside hip toward the center of the circle so that your inside leg stays on the circle.

4. Glide slightly, after uncrossing your legs.

5.
Step over your inside
skate (toward the center of the circle) with
your outside skate again.

6. Again, rotate
your inside hip
toward the
center of the
circle and
uncross
your legs.

7. Maintain
upper body
positioning
and glide
after uncross-
ing your legs.

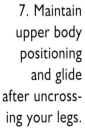

Backward Crossovers

Backward crossovers should always be practiced going around a circle. Crossing—or scissoring—your legs requires a strong push with the outside leg, followed by a strong pull with the inside leg to maintain the circle as the outside skate passes in front of the inside skate. Step out from behind with your inside skate and set it down away from the outside skate and toward the center of the circle; reach for the center of the circle with your inside skate as you uncross your legs. Remember, your outside skate is never lifted off the ice during backward crossovers. Maintaining the proper upper body positioning throughout is crucial to accomplishing crossovers.

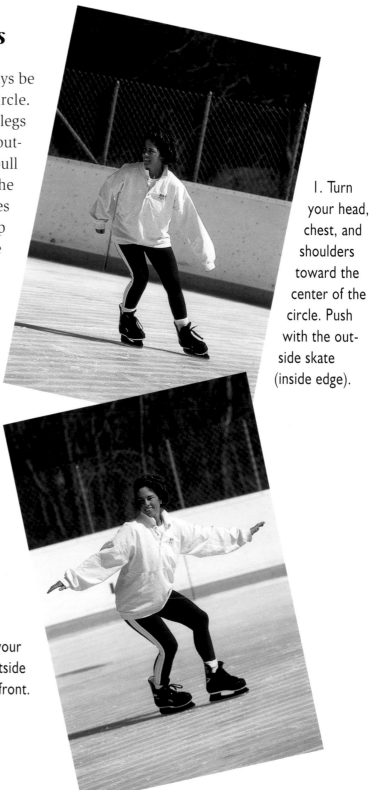

1. Turn your head, chest, and shoulders toward the center of the circle. Push with the outside skate (inside edge).

2. Now pull yourself around with your inside skate (outside edge) as your outside skate crosses in front.

3. Keep pulling with your inside skate as your legs cross.

4. Continue the pull with your inside skate until your legs are fully crossed. Notice how your inside skate has remained flat and on its outside edge throughout the pull.

5. Begin to step the inside skate out from behind the outside skate.

7. Pull with your inside skate as your outside skate crosses in front of you.

6. Push hard with the inside edge of the outside skate.

8. Begin to step out from behind with your inside skate.

9. Reach for the center of the circle with your inside skate as you push with your outside skate.

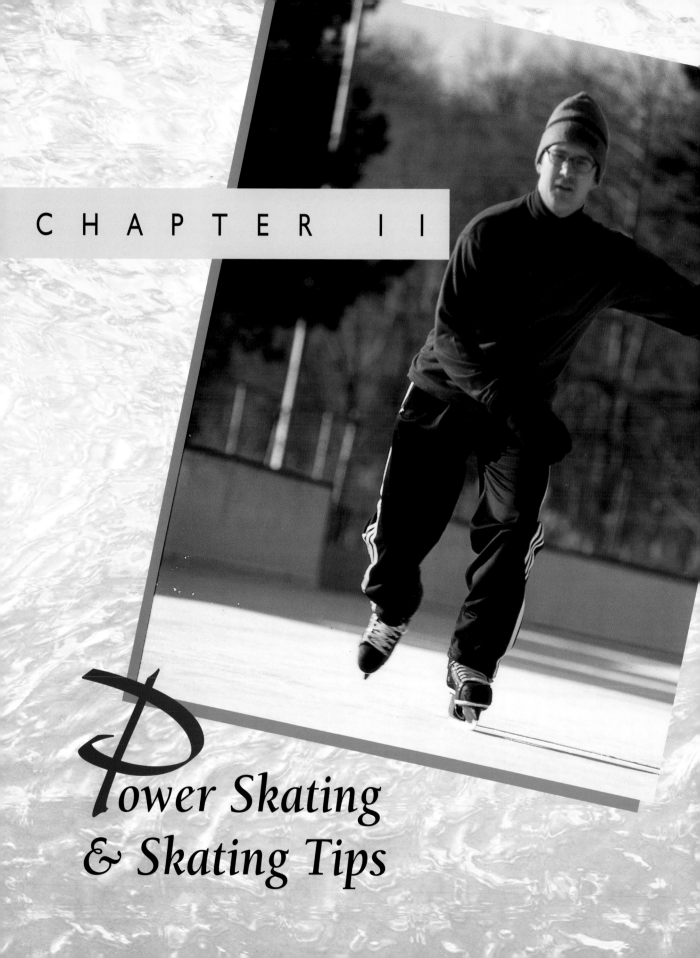

CHAPTER 11

Power Skating
& Skating Tips

Several important steps will maximize the power derived from each skating stride. In full stride a skilled skater only has one skate on the ice 99% of the time! In a fast sprint one skate starts its push while the other skate is being recovered, that is, is picked up at the end of its push and set down under the body. The skate being recovered begins its push the moment it's set down under the body. At most, the skates are on the ice together for a split second. In a slower (but efficient and powerful) stride the leading skate glides while the other skate is recovered. As soon as the recovered skate is set down, it becomes the gliding skate, and the original gliding skate makes its push.

There should be very little width between the places where the skates push off from under the body. In fact, in full stride your skates should replace each other in almost the same place under your body each time you push and recover. New skaters typically skate with a wider stance and therefore some of their push is "used up" already in width between their skates.

To maximize your power you must bend deeply at the knees. Bending forward from the waist is necessary as well, to keep your balance when moving forward quickly. By bending at the waist and knees you are able to get the fullest leg and body extension with each push.

To get a powerful start, stand perpendicular to the direction you will travel. This puts the edge of your starting skate sideways and maximizes its pushing power.

Finally, use your upper body and arms much like a runner would to draw the most power from each stride. Your arms should swing in the direction of the forward, gliding skate. This helps push you along and centers your weight over the forward skate.

Look for the attributes of a powerful stride (and a powerful start) in the following photos.

1.
Getting ready for a powerful start. Notice how we are turned almost perpendicular to our line of travel.

4. Arms crossed fully to the other side

2. A powerful start with full-leg extension and arms on the side of the lead skate

5. Full extension as soon as the lead skate is recovered and touches the ice. Arms swing in the direction of the lead skate.

3. The initial pushing skate is starting its recovery as the initial lead skate is in mid-push. Move arms to the other side.

The following photos show arm and upper body positions over the leading (gliding) skate. They show a slower stride with a longer glide time on the leading skate than the previous five photos.

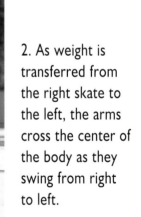

1. Arms are on the right side of the body when the right skate leads.

2. As weight is transferred from the right skate to the left, the arms cross the center of the body as they swing from right to left.

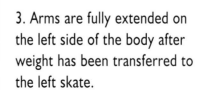

3. Arms are fully extended on the left side of the body after weight has been transferred to the left skate.

The Crossunder

In both forward and backward crossovers crossing the legs is initiated with the push from the outside skate. The crossunder, or push from the inside skate as the legs are crossing, is a strong way to derive speed and holding power (in a tight turn) from your crossovers. This push is often neglected because it is subtle and difficult to concentrate on when you are learning crossovers. The crossunder push is always done with the outside edge of the inside skate as the legs cross, and should extend the inside leg into a fully extended (and crossed) position.

Forward Crossunder

2. ...and fully extends the inside skate behind the other leg.

1.
The inside leg starts the crossunder push as the outside skate crosses...

Backward Crossunder

1. In backward crossovers the inside leg starts its crossunder here after it has "reached" for the center of the circle.

2. The inside leg in mid-push (crossunder) as the outside skate is passing in front

3. The inside skate fully extended (to the left, in the photo) and on its outside edge behind the outside skate from the crossunder push

Acknowledgments

First and foremost, I'd like to thank photographer Bruce Curtis and fellow instructor and author Cam Millar for making this book possible. I am also deeply grateful to Caroline Roberts; writing coach Lynn Harris; and Carol Anne Herlihy, at the law firm of Kellner, Chehebar and Deveney. Also, I'd like to thank the following models and skaters for their patience and sense of humor during photo shoots: Wendy Tzou, Kathy Berliner, Virginia Pierrepont, Susie Kirk, Betsy Gahagan, Andy Wagner, Donna Lasser, and Linda Sheridan. Finally, thank you to Scott Kelliher and Beth at Blades-Chelsea Piers, to Phil and Jose at 3rd St. Skate in Brooklyn, and to all the skating students and instructors with whom I've worked.

Index